Meerkats Are Awesome!

by Lisa J. Amstutz

Consultant: Jackie Gai, DVM
Captive Wildlife Veterinarian

CAPSTONE PRESS
a capstone imprint

A+ Books are published by Capstone Press,
1710 Roe Crest Drive, North Mankato, Minnesota 56003
www.capstonepub.com

Library of Congress Cataloging-in-Publication Data
Amstutz, Lisa J., author.
  Meerkats are awesome! / by Lisa J. Amstutz.
    pages cm. — (A+ books. Awesome African animals)
  Summary: "Describes the characteristics, habitat, behavior, life cycle, and threats to meerkats living in the wild
of Africa"—Provided by publisher.
  Audience: Ages 5-8.
  Audience: K to grade 3.
  Includes bibliographical references and index.
  ISBN 978-1-4914-1763-8 (library binding)
  ISBN 978-1-4914-1769-0 (paperback)
  ISBN 978-1-4914-1775-1 (eBook PDF)
1. Meerkat—Juvenile literature. 2. Animals—Africa—Juvenile literature. I. Title.

QL737.C235A47 2015
599.74'2—dc23   2014023672

Editorial Credits
Erika Shores and Mari Bolte, editors; Cynthia Della-Rovere, designer; Svetlana Zhurkin, media researcher;
Morgan Walters, production specialist

Photo Credits
Alamy: Adam Seward, 20 (bottom); Dreamstime: Alta Oosthuizen, 6, Manit321, 10, Schnappschusshelge, 16
(bottom); Getty Images: Barcroft Media/Burrard-Lucas, 13; iStockphotos: GlobalP, cover (top right), 1 (top),
18 (top); Minden Pictures: Vincent Grafhorst, 12; Newscom: Moonshine Media/Jeremy Jowell, 20—21, 22,
Photoshot/NHPA/Martin Harvey, 28—29, Photoshot/NHPA/Nigel J. Dennis, 17, Robert Harding/Ann &
Steve Toon, 26—27; Shutterstock: Aaron Amat, cover (top left, bottom), back cover, 1 (bottom), 32, Alfredo
Cerra, 14, belizar, 19, Bildagentur Zoonar GmbH, 23, Black Sheep Media (grass), back cover and throughout,
e2dan, 29 (bottom), EcoPrint, 16 (top), 25 (top), Fiona Ayerst, 8—9, Kristina Stasiuliene, 15, MartinMaritz, 25
(middle), Michael Wick, 24—25, Photodynamic, 5, santol, 11, spirit of America (African landscape background),
throughout, Super Prin, 7 (back), Tina Rencelj, 18 (bottom), Tristan Tan, cover (top middle), 7 (front), 26
(middle), Valentyna Chukhlyebova, 4

Note to Parents, Teachers, and Librarians
This Awesome African Animals book uses full color photographs and a nonfiction format to
introduce the concept of meerkats. *Meerkats Are Awesome!* is designed to be read aloud to a
pre-reader or to be read independently by an early reader. Photographs help listeners and early
readers understand the text and concepts discussed. The book encourages further learning by
including the following sections: Table of Contents, Glossary, Read More, Internet Sites, and Index.
Early readers may need assistance using these features.

Printed in China by Nordica.
0914/CA21401520
092014   008470NORDS15

Table of Contents

Living in Africa

Pop! A furry head pokes out of a hole. Then another, and another. Soon there's a whole mob … of meerkats!

A meerkat is a mammal. It belongs to the mongoose family. It stands as tall as your knee and weighs about 2 pounds (0.9 kilogram).

Meerkat fur is light brown with dark stripes. The fur matches the dry soil. Meerkats' fur hides them from predators. Dark rings around their eyes act like sunglasses in the bright sunshine.

Africa

Where Meerkats Live

Meerkats live on the plains of Africa. The ground is dry and rocky. Grasses and shrubs dot the land. The sun blazes hot. Summer days can reach 104 degrees Fahrenheit (40 degrees Celsius). It is hard to keep cool in Africa. But meerkats do a good job.

Meerkats pant like dogs to cool down. Their coats shed heat well. They dig up cool sand and lie on it. Or they cool off in their burrows underground.

Digging Deep

Meerkats live in burrows. Sometimes they share them with other animals, such as ground squirrels or yellow mongooses.

Burrows are full of long underground tunnels and rooms. The many exits are called bolt holes. Above ground, meerkats stay near these holes. They dive in when danger is near.

Meerkats dig burrows with their long, sharp claws. They fold their ears back so sand can't get in. They are fast diggers. A meerkat can move its own weight in sand in just seconds.

On the Menu

Meerkats dig for food too. They eat insects, spiders, and worms. And scorpions are always on the menu! The scorpion's poison doesn't hurt meerkats.

Meerkats also eat rodents, lizards, eggs, and plants. They spend up to eight hours a day eating. They rarely drink water. They get enough water from the food they eat.

Growing Families

Female meerkats give birth one to four times a year. Two to five pups are in each litter. Pups are born hairless and blind. They stay in the burrow for four weeks, drinking their mother's milk. Then they start eating chewed-up food.

The pups huddle to keep warm.
They wrestle and play. Meerkat pups
learn to be part of the mob.

Life in the Mob

Up to 30 meerkats live in a mob. They work together to find food and stay safe. The members groom each other to remove ticks and insects. Each mob has a large territory. The mob keeps other meerkats out.

Everyone in the mob has a job to do. Adult meerkats take turns as lookouts. The lookouts find high spots to watch for danger. They warn the mob with a shrill bark when a predator is near.

Babysitters keep pups safe
while their mothers hunt. Teachers
help pups learn to find food.

Desert Dangers

Meerkats face many dangers.
Predators like hawks, snakes, and jackals
hunt them. Pups can die if they get
wet and cold. And humans sometimes
damage the areas where meerkats live.

A lookout stands on its hind legs. It uses its tail for balance. The tail is almost as long as its body. Meerkats see very well. They can spot a hawk 1,000 feet (300 meters) away.

Don't mess with the mob! Meerkats team up to chase away cobras, foxes, and other small predators. If cornered, meerkats will even attack a jackal. Dust flies as they jump, growl, and bite.

When a meerkat gets hurt, the others carry it to the burrow. They feed it and keep it warm. This teamwork is just one reason why meerkats are awesome animals!

29

Glossary

burrow (BUHR-oh)—to dig a hole; a burrow can also be a hole in the ground that an animal makes

groom (GROOM)—to clean and make an animal look neat

litter (LIT-ur)—a group of animals born at the same time to one mother

mammal (MAM-uhl)—a warm–blooded animal that breathes air; mammals have hair or fur; female mammals feed milk to their young

mob (MOB)—a group of meerkats that live together

pant (PANT)—to breathe quickly with an open mouth; some animals pant to cool off

plains (PLAYNS)—a large, flat area of land with few trees

predator (PRED-uh-tur)—an animal that hunts other animals for food

territory (TER-uh-tor-ee)—the land on which an animal grazes or hunts for food, and raises its young

Read More

Ganeri, Anita. *A Day in the Life: Desert Animals*. Chicago: Heinemann Library, 2011.

Harasymiw, Therese. *Animals that Live in the Grasslands: Meerkats*. New York: Gareth Stevens Publishing, 2011.

Marsh, Laura. *National Geographic Kids: Meerkats*. Washington, D.C.: National Geographic Society, 2012.

Internet Sites

FactHound offers a safe, fun way to find Internet sites related to this book. All of the sites on FactHound have been researched by our staff.

Here's all you do:
Visit *www.facthound.com*
Type in this code: 9781491417638

Super-cool stuff!

Check out projects, games and lots more at
www.capstonekids.com

Critical Thinking Using the Common Core

1. How are meerkat mobs similar to your family? How are they different? (Key Ideas and Details)

2. Look at all the pictures of meerkat dens. Describe how they would look in a different part of the world, such as the Midwest or Antarctica. (Integration of Knowledge and Ideas)

3. Where else would a meerkat's coat blend in? (Integration of Knowledge and Ideas)

Index